D1577570

27911

821

This book is to be returned on or before
the last date stamped below.

	16 FEB 2008
MAY 1992	
18 MAY 1992	
5 OCT 1992	
-8 DEC 1995	
2 6 NOV 1996	
2 0 MAR 2000	WITHDRAWN
-7 JUL 2000	
6/2004	
1 DEC 2006	
16 FEB 2008	LIBREX

27911.

STOCKPORT GRAMMAR SCHOOL
LIBRARY

Poetry of the
First World War

'I don't think these shell-shocked war poems will move our grandchildren greatly –' Sir Henry Newbolt, 1924.

POETRY
OF THE FIRST
WORLD WAR

'*The hell where youth and laughter go*'

Dedicated to
Lance Corporal Bert Bennett of the Bedfordshire Regiment
and
Leutnant Hubert Sulzbach

Selected by
EDWARD HUDSON

Wayland

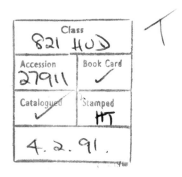

Class	
821 HUD	
Accession	Book Card
27911	✓
Catalogued	Stamped
✓	HT
4.2.91.	

Designer: David Armitage
Editor: Susannah Foreman

First published in 1988 by
Wayland (Publishers) Ltd
61 Western Road, Hove,
East Sussex, BN3 1JD

This selection © Copyright 1988 Edward Hudson

Typeset, printed and bound in the UK
by Butler and Tanner Ltd, Frome and London

British Library Cataloguing in Publication Data
Poetry of the First World War.
   1. Poetry in English, 1900–1945. Special
   subjects: World War 1 – Anthologies
   I. Hudson, Edward
   821'.912'080358

   ISBN 1–85210–667–0

CONTENTS

1917

1918

1919 and beyond

Preface

Edward Hudson does well to remind us of Sir Henry Newbolt's prophecy: 'I don't think these shell-shocked war poems will move our grandchildren greatly.' Wilfred Owen was troubled by a similar thought when he wrote: 'How the Future will forget the dead in war.' Clearly both were wrong, but it is also clear that they and their contemporaries must have read these poems with eyes very different from our own; eyes bombarded with the images of 1914–1918, as their ears were bombarded at first or second hand by 'the monstrous anger of the guns ... the stuttering rifles' rapid rattle'. Many of the poets of that period saw it as their task to bombard their readers with the sights, sounds, smells that assaulted the senses of those in front–lines many at home could not imagine. Owen wrote to his mother in October 1918: 'I came out in order to help these boys – directly by leading them as well as an officer can; indirectly, by watching their sufferings that I may speak of them as well as a pleader can.' He must *watch* that he may *plead*; he must *see* that he may *speak*. As he says in the draft Preface to his poems: 'All a poet can do today is warn. That is why the true Poets will be truthful.'

He and the other 'true Poets' bore witness well enough to disprove Newbolt's prophecy, but time has a way of obscuring the detail of texts as of canvasses. Both need to be 'cleaned' from time to time if they are to make their full impact on a new generation of readers or viewers. And that is what Edward Hudson has done so skilfully in this anthology. By setting the poems of 1914–1918 in a visual context, he dramatically sharpens our response to them. See, for example, how the smiling faces increase the voltage of Siegfried Sassoon's 'Does it Matter?'

No one coming to such poems in the setting Edward Hudson has given them could ever 'forget the dead in war', or the survivors. For this, their poets would be grateful to him – as I am, and as many others will be.

Jon Stallworthy

GLIMPSE

W. N. Hodgson

I saw you fooling often in the tents
With fair dishevelled hair and laughing lips,
And frolic elf lights in your careless eyes,
As who had never known the taste of tears
Or the world's sorrow. Then on the march one night,
Halted beneath the stars I heard the sound
Of talk and laughter, and glanced back to see
If you were there. But you stood far apart
and silent, bowed upon your rifle butt,
And gazed into the night as one who sees.
I marked the drooping lips and fathomless eyes
And knew you brooded on immortal things.

Written in June 1914

ENGLAND TO HER SONS   W. N. Hodgson

Sons of mine, I hear you thrilling
To the trumpet call of war;
Gird ye then, I give you freely
As I gave your sires before,
All the noblest of the children I in love and anguish bore.

Free in service, wise in justice,
Fearing but dishonour's breath;
Steeled to suffer uncomplaining
Loss and failure, pain and death;
Strong in faith that sees the issue and in hope that triumpheth.

Go, and may the God of battles
You in His good guidance keep:
And if He in wisdom giveth
Unto His beloved sleep,
I accept it nothing asking, save a little space to weep.

Written in August 1914

From *MEN WHO MARCH AWAY*   **Thomas Hardy**

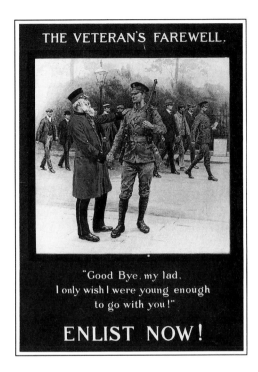

In our heart of hearts believing
Victory crowns the just,
And that braggarts must
Surely bite the dust,
Press we to the field ungrieving,
in our heart of hearts believing
Victory crowns the just.

Hence the faith and fire within us
Men who march away
Ere the barn-cocks say
Night is growing grey,
Leaving all that here can win us;
Hence the faith and fire within us
Men who march away.

Written in September 1914

FOR THE FALLEN
(September 1914)

Laurence Binyon

With proud thanksgiving, a mother for her children,
England mourns for her dead across the sea.
Flesh of her flesh they were, spirit of her spirit,
Fallen in the cause of the free.

Solemn the drums thrill: Death august and royal
Sings sorrow up into immortal spheres.
There is music in the midst of desolation
And glory that shines upon our tears.

They went with songs to the battle, they were young,
Straight of limb, true of eye, steady and aglow.
They were staunch to the end against odds uncounted:
They fell with their faces to the foe.

They shall grow not old, as we that are left grow old:
Age shall not weary them, nor the years condemn.
At the going down of the sun and in the morning
We will remember them.

They mingle not with their laughing comrades again;
They sit no more at familiar tables of home;
They have no lot in our labour of the day-time;
They sleep beyond England's foam.

But where our desires are and our hopes profound,
Felt as a well-spring that is hidden from sight,
To the innermost heart of their own land they are known
As the stars are known to the Night;

As the stars that shall be bright when we are dust,
Moving in marches upon the heavenly plain;
As the stars that are starry in the time of our darkness,
To the end, to the end they remain.

Published in September 1914

We ate our breakfast lying on our backs,
Because the shells were screeching overhead.
I bet a rasher to a loaf of bread
That Hull United would beat Halifax
When Jimmy Stainthorp played full-back instead
Of Billy Bradford. Ginger raised his head
And cursed, and took the bet; and dropt back dead.
We ate our breakfast lying on our backs,
Because the shells were screeching overhead.

Published in October 1914

Now, God be thanked Who has matched us with His hour,
And caught our youth and wakened us from sleeping,
With hand made sure, clear eye, and sharpened power,
To turn, as swimmers into cleanness leaping,
Glad from a world grown old and cold and weary,
Leave the sick hearts that honour could not move,
And half-men, and their dirty songs and dreary,
And all the little emptiness of love!

Oh! we who have known shame, we have found release there,
Where there's no ill, no grief, but sleep has mending
Naught broken save this body, lost but breath;
Nothing to shake the laughing heart's long peace there
But only agony, and that has ending;
And the worst friend and enemy is but Death.

Written in December 1914

THE SOLDIER **Rupert Brooke**

If I should die, think only this of me;
That there's some corner of a foreign field
That is for ever England. There shall be
In that rich earth a richer dust concealed;
A dust whom England bore, shaped, made aware,
Gave, once, her flowers to love, her ways to roam,
A body of England's, breathing English air,
Washed by the rivers, blest by suns of home.

And think, this heart, all evil shed away,
A pulse in the eternal mind, no less
Gives somewhere back the thoughts by England given;
Her sights and sounds; dreams happy as her day;
And laughter, learnt of friends; and gentleness,
In hearts at peace, under an English heaven.

Written in December 1914

A LISTENING POST

R. E. Vernède

The sun's a red ball in the oak
And all the grass is grey with dew,
A while ago a blackbird spoke –
He didn't know the world's askew

And yonder rifleman and I
Wait here behind the misty trees
To shoot the first man that goes by,
Our rifles ready on our knees.

How could he know that if we fail
The world may lie in chains for years
And England be a bygone tale
And right be wrong, and laughter tears?

Strange that this bird sits there and sings
While we must only sit and plan –
Who are so much the higher thing –
The murder of our fellow man . . .

But maybe God will cause to be –
Who brought forth sweetness from the strong –
Out of our discords harmony
Sweeter than the bird's song.

Written before March 1915

'I TRACKED A DEAD MAN DOWN A TRENCH'   W. S. Lyon

I tracked a dead man down a trench,
I knew not he was dead.
They told me he had gone that way,
And there his foot-marks led.

The trench was long and close and curved,
It seemed without an end;
And as I threaded each new bay
I thought to see my friend.

I went there stooping to the ground.
For, should I raise my head,
Death watched to spring; and how should then
A dead man find the dead?

At last I saw his back. He crouched
As still as still could be,
And when I called his name aloud
He did not answer me.

The floor-way of the trench was wet
Where he was crouching dead:
The water of the pool was brown,
And round him it was red.

I stole up softly where he stayed
With head hung down all slack,
And on his shoulders laid my hands
And drew him gently back.

And then, as I had guessed, I saw
His head, and how the crown –
I saw then why he crouched so still,
And why his head hung down.

Written in April 1915

The naked earth is warm with Spring,
   And with green grass and bursting trees
Leans to the sun's gaze glorying,
   And quivers in the sunny breeze;
And life is colour and warmth and light,
   And a striving evermore for these;
And he is dead who will not fight;
   And who dies fighting has increase.

The fighting man shall from the sun
    Take warmth, and life from the glowing earth;
Speed with the light-foot winds to run,
    And with the trees to newer birth;
And find, when fighting shall be done,
    Great rest, and fullness after dearth.

All the bright company of Heaven
    Hold him in their high comradeship,
The Dog-Star, and the Sisters Seven,
    Orion's Belt and sworded hip.

The woodland trees that stand together,
    They stand to him each one a friend;
They gently speak in the windy weather;
    They guide to valley and ridge's end.

The kestrel hovering by day,
    And the little owls that call by night,
Bid him be swift and keen as they,
    As keen of ear, as swift of sight.

The blackbird sings to him, 'Brother, brother,
    If this be the last song you shall sing,
Sing well, for you may not sing another;
    Brother, sing'.

In dreary doubtful, waiting hours,
    Before the brazen frenzy starts,
The horses show him nobler powers;
    O patient eyes, courageous hearts!

And when the burning moment breaks,
    And all things else are out of mind,
And only joy of battle takes
    Him by the throat, and makes him blind,

Through joy and blindness he shall know,
    Not caring much to know, that still
Nor lead nor steel shall reach him, so
    That it be not the Destined Will.

The thundering line of battle stands,
    And in the air death moans and sings;
But Day shall clasp him with strong hands,
    And Night shall fold him in soft wings.

Written in April 1915

God heard the embattled nations sing and shout
'Gott strafe England!' and 'God save the King!'
God this, God that, and God the other thing –
'Good God!' said God, 'I've got my work cut out.'

Published in June 1915

'WHEN YOU SEE MILLIONS OF THE MOUTHLESS DEAD'   **Charles Sorley**

When you see millions of the mouthless dead
Across your dreams in pale battalions go,
Say not soft things as other men have said,
That you'll remember. For you need not so.
Give them not praise. For, deaf, how should they know
It is not curses heaped on each gashed head?
Nor tears. Their blind eyes see not your tears flow.
Nor honour. It is easy to be dead.
Say only this, 'They are dead.' Then add thereto,
'Yet many a better one has died before.'
Then, scanning all the o'ercrowded mass, should you
Perceive one face that you loved heretofore,
It is a spook. None wears the face you knew.
Great death has made all his for evermore.

Written in 1915

BACK

W. W. Gibson

They ask me where I've been,
And what I've done and seen.
But what can I reply
Who know it wasn't I,
But someone just like me,
Who went across the sea
And with my head and hands
Killed men in foreign lands ...
Though I must bear the blame,
Because he bore my name.

Published in July 1915

BACK TO REST   W. N. Hodgson

A leaping wind from England,
The skies without a stain,
Clean cut against the morning
Slim poplars after rain,
The foolish noise of sparrows
And starlings in a wood –
After the grime of battle
We know that these are good.

Death whining down from Heaven,
Death roaring from the ground,
Death stinking in the nostril,
Death shrill in every sound,
Doubting we charged and conquered –
Hopeless we struck and stood.
Now when the fight is ended
We know that it was good.

We that have seen the strongest
Cry like a beaten child,
The sanest eyes unholy,
The cleanest hands defiled,
We that have known the heart blood
Less than the lees of wine,
We that have seen men broken,
We know man is divine.

Written in September 1915

THE REDEEMER   **Siegfried Sassoon**

Darkness: the rain sluiced down; the mire was deep;
It was past twelve on a mid-winter night,
When peaceful folk in beds lay snug asleep;
There, with much work to do before the light,
We lugged our clay-sucked boots as best we might
Along the trench; sometimes a bullet sang,
And droning shells burst with a hollow bang;
We were soaked, chilled and wretched, every one;
Darkness: the distant wink of a huge gun.

I turned in the black ditch, loathing the storm;
A rocket fizzed and burned with blanching flare,
And lit the face of what had been a form
Floundering in mirk. He stood before me there;
I say that He was Christ; stiff in the glare,
And leaning forward from His burdening task,
Both arms supporting it; His eyes on mine
Stared for the woeful head that seemed a mask
Of mortal pain in Hell's unholy shine.

No thorny crown, only a woollen cap
He wore – an English soldier, white and strong,
Who loved his time like any simple chap,
Good days of work and sport and homely song;
Now he has learned that nights are very long,
And dawn a watching of the windowed sky.
But to the end, unjudging, he'll endure
Horror and pain, not uncontent to die
That Lancaster on Lune may stand secure.

He faced me, reeling in his weariness,
Shouldering his load of planks, so hard to bear.
I say that He was Christ, who wrought to bless
All groping things with freedom bright as air,
And with His mercy washed and made them fair.
Then the flame sank, and all grew black as pitch,
While we began to struggle along the ditch;
And someone flung his burden in the muck,
Mumbling: 'O Christ Almighty, now I'm stuck!'

Written in November 1915

IN FLANDERS FIELDS   **John McCrae**

In Flanders fields the poppies blow
Between the crosses, row on row
That mark our place; and in the sky
The larks, still bravely singing, fly
Scarce heard amid the guns below.

We are the Dead. Short days ago
We lived, felt dawn, saw sunset glow,
Loved and were loved, and now we lie
In Flanders fields.

Take up our quarrel with the foe:
To you from failing hands we throw
The torch; be yours to hold it high.
If ye break faith with us who die
We shall not sleep, though poppies grow
In Flanders fields.

Published in December 1915

PRAYER FOR THOSE ON THE STAFF

Julian Grenfell

Fighting in mud we turn to Thee,
In these dread times of battle, Lord,
To keep us safe, if so may be,
From shrapnel, snipers, shell, and sword.

But not on us, for we are men
Of meaner clay, who fight in clay,
But on the Staff, the Upper Ten,
Depends the issue of the Day.

The Staff is working with its brains,
While we are sitting in the trench;
The Staff the universe ordains
(Subject to Thee and General French.)

God help the Staff – especially
The young ones, many of them sprung
From our high aristocracy;
Their task is hard, and they are young.

O Lord, who mad'st all things to be,
And madest some things very good,
Please keep the extra A.D.C.
From horrid scenes, and sight of blood.

See that his eggs are newly laid,
Not tinged as some of them – with green;
And let no nasty draughts invade
The windows of his limousine.

When he forgets to buy the bread,
When there are no more minerals,
Preserve his smooth well–oiled head
From wrath of caustic Generals.

O Lord, who mad'st all things to be,
And hatest nothing thou have made,
Please keep the extra A.D.C.
Out of the sun and in the shade.

Written in 1915

RENDEZVOUS   **Alan Seeger**

I have a rendezvous with Death
At some disputed barricade,
When Spring comes back with rustling shade
And apple-blossoms fill the air –
I have a rendezvous with Death
When Spring brings back blue days and fair.

It may be he shall take my hand
And lead me into his dark land
And close my eyes and quench my breath –
It may be I shall pass him still.
I have a rendezvous with Death
On some scarred slope of battered hill
When Spring comes round again this year
And the first meadow–flowers appear.

God knows 'twere better to be deep
Pillowed in silk and scented down,
Where love throbs out in blissful sleep,
Pulse nigh to pulse, and breath to breath,
Where hushed awakenings are dear . . .
But I've a rendezous with Death
At midnight in some flaming town,
When Spring trips north again this year,
And I to my pledged word am true,
I shall not fail that rendezvous.

Written between January and February 1916

THE NIGHT PATROL   **Arthur Graeme West**

Over the top! The wire's thin here, unbarbed
Plain rusty coils, not staked, and low enough:
Full of old tins, though – 'When you're through, all three,
Aim quarter left for fifty yards or so,
Then straight for that new piece of German wire;
See if it's thick, and listen for a while
For sounds of working; don't run any risks;
About an hour; now over!'
And we placed
Our hands on the topmost sand-bags, leapt, and stood
A second with curved backs, then crept to the wire,
Wormed ourselves tinkling through, glanced back, and dropped
The sodden ground was splashed with shallow pools,
And tufts of crackling cornstalks, two years old,
No man had reaped, and patches of spring grass,
Half-seen, as rose and sank the flares, were strewn
With the wrecks of our attack: the bandoliers,
Packs, rifles, bayonets, belts, and haversacks,
Shell fragments, and the huge whole forms of shells
Shot fruitlessly – and everywhere the dead.

Only the dead were always present – present
As a vile sickly smell of rottenness;
The rustling stubble and the early grass,
The slimy pools – the dead men stank through all,
Pungent and sharp; as bodies loomed before,
And as we passed, they stank; then dulled away
To that vague foetor, all encompassing,
Infecting earth and air. They lay, all clothed,
Each in some new and piteous attitude
That we well marked to guide us back: as he,
Outside our wire, that lay on his back and crossed
His legs Crusader-wise; I smiled at that,
And thought on Elia and his Temple Church.
From him, at quarter left, lay a small corpse,
Down in a hollow, huddled as in bed,
That one of us put his hand on unawares.
Next was a bunch of half a dozen men
All blown to bits, an archipelago
Of corrupt fragments, vexing to us three,
Who had no light to see by, save the flares.
On such a trail, so lit, for ninety yards
We crawled on belly and elbows, till we saw,
Instead of lumpish dead before our eyes,
The stakes and crosslines of the German wire.
We lay in shelter of the last dead man,
Ourselves as dead, and heard their shovels ring
Turning the earth, then talk and cough at times.
A sentry fired and a machine-gun spat;
They shot a flare above us; when it fell
And spluttered out in the pools of No Man's Land,
We turned and crawled past the remembered dead:
Past him and him, and them and him, until,
For he lay some way apart, we caught the scent
Of the Crusader and slid past his legs,
And through the wire and home, and got our rum.

Written in March 1916

Three hours ago he blundered up the trench,
Sliding and poising, groping with his boots;
Sometimes he tripped and lurched against the walls
With hands that pawed the sodden bags of chalk.
He couldn't see the man who walked in front;
Only he heard the drum and rattle of feet
Stepping along barred trench boards, often splashing
Wretchedly where the sludge was ankle-deep.

Voices would grunt 'Keep to your right – make way!'
When squeezing past some men from the front-line:
White faces peered, puffing a point of red;
Candles and braziers glinted through the chinks
And curtain-flaps of dug-outs; then the gloom
Swallowed his sense of sight; he stooped and swore
Because a sagging wire had caught his neck.

A flare went up; the shining whiteness spread
And flickered upward, showing nimble rats
And mounds of glimmering sandbags, bleached with rain;
Then the slow silver moment died in dark.

The wind came posting by with chilly gusts
And buffeting at corners, piping thin.
And dreary through the crannies; rifle-shots
Would split and crack and sing along the night,
And shells came calmly through the drizzling air
To burst with hollow bang below the hill.

Three hours ago he stumbled up the trench;
Now he will never walk that road again:
He must be carried back, a jolting lump
Beyond all need of tenderness and care.
He was a young man with a meagre wife
And two small children in a Midland town;
He showed their photographs to all his mates,
And they considered him a decent chap
Who did his work and hadn't much to say,
And always laughed at other people's jokes
Because he hadn't any of his own.

That night when he was busy at his job
Of piling bags along the parapet,
He thought how slow time went, stamping his feet
And blowing on his fingers, pinched with cold.
He thought of getting back by half-past twelve,
And tot of rum to send him warm to sleep
In draughty dug-out frowsty with the fumes
Of coke, and full of snoring weary men.

He pushed another bag along the top,
Craning his body outward; then a flare
Gave one white glimpse of No Man's Land and wire;
And as he dropped his head the instant split
His startled life with lead, and all went out.

Written in March 1916

As the team's head-brass flashed out on the turn
The lovers disappeared into the wood.
I sat among the boughs of the fallen elm
That strewed an angle of the fallow, and
Watched the plough narrowing a yellow square
Of charlock. Every time the horses turned
Instead of treading me down, the ploughman leaned
Upon the handles to say or ask a word,
About the weather, next about the war.
Scraping the share he faced towards the wood,
And screwed along the furrow till the brass flashed
Once more.

The blizzard felled the elm whose crest
I sat in, by a woodpecker's round hole,
The ploughman said. 'When will they take it away?'
'When the war's over.' So the talk began –
One minute and an interval of ten,
A minute more and the same interval.
'Have you been out?' 'No.' 'And don't want to, perhaps?'
'If I could only come back again, I should.
I could spare an arm. I shouldn't want to lose
A leg. If I should lose my head, why, so,
I should want nothing more . . . Have many gone
From here?' 'Yes.' 'Many Lost?' 'Yes a good few.

Only two teams work on the farm this year.
One of my mates is dead. The second day
In France they killed him. It was back in March,
The very night of the blizzard, too. Now if
He had stayed here we should have moved the tree.'
'And I should not have sat here. Everything
Would have been different. For it would have been
Another world.' 'Ay, and a better, though
If we could see all all might seem good.' Then
The lovers came out of the wood again:
The horses started and for the last time
I watched the clods crumble and topple over
After the ploughshare and the stumbling team.

Written in May 1916

TWO VOICES   **David Westcott Brown**

'The roads are all torn', 'but the sun's in the sky,'
'The houses are waste'; 'but the day is all fair,'
'There's death in the air'; 'and the larks are on high,'
'Though we die –'; 'It is spring-time, what do we care?'

'The Gardens are rank'; 'but the grass is still green,'
'The orchards are shot-torn'; 'There's bloom on the trees,'
'There's war all around'; 'Yet is nature serene,'
'There's danger'; 'we'll bear it, fanned by the breeze.'

'Some are wounded'; 'they rest, and their glory is known,'
'Some are killed'; 'there's peace for them under the sod,'
'Men's homes are in peril'; 'their souls are their own,'
'The bullets are near us'; 'not nearer than God.'

Written in May 1916

BEFORE ACTION   **W. N. Hodgson**

By all the glories of the day
   And the cool evening's benison,
By that last sunset touch that lay
   Upon the hills when day was done,
By beauty lavishly outpoured
   And blessings carelessly received,
By all the days that I have lived
   Make me a soldier, Lord.

By all of all man's hopes and fears,
   And all the wonders poets sing,
The laughter of unclouded years,
   And every sad and lovely thing;
By the romantic ages stored
   With high endeavour that was his,
By all his mad catastrophes
   Make me a man, O Lord.

I, that on my familiar hill
   Saw with uncomprehending eyes
A hundred of Thy sunsets spill
   Their fresh and sanguine sacrifice,
Ere the sun swings his noonday sword
   Must say good-bye to all of this;—
By all delights that I shall miss,
   Help me to die, O Lord.

Published in June 1916

BREAK OF DAY IN THE TRENCHES

Isaac Rosenberg

The darkness crumbles away –
It is the same old druid Time as ever.
Only a live thing leaps in my hand –
A queer sardonic rat –
As I pull the parapet's poppy
To stick behind my ear.
Droll rat, they would shoot you if they knew
Your cosmopolitan sympathies.
(And God knows what antipathies).
Now you have touched this English hand
You will do the same to a German –
Soon, no doubt, if it be your pleasure
To cross the sleeping green between.
It seems you inwardly grin as you pass
Strong eyes, fine limbs, haughty athletes
Less chanced than you for life,

Bonds to the whims of murder,
Sprawled in the bowels of the earth,
The torn fields of France.
What do you see in our eyes
At the shrieking iron and flame
Hurled through still heavens?
What quaver – what heart aghast?
Poppies whose roots are in man's veins
Drop, and are ever dropping;
But mine in my ear is safe,
Just a little white with the dust.

Written in June 1916

We'd gained our first objective hours before
While dawn broke like a face with blinking eyes,
Pallid, unshaved and thirsty, blind with smoke.
Things seemed all right at first. We held their line,
With bombers posted, Lewis guns well placed,
And clink of shovels deepening the shallow trench.
The place was rotten with dead; green clumsy legs
High-booted, sprawled and grovelled along the saps;
And trunks, face downward, in the sucking mud,
Wallowed like trodden sand-bags loosely filled;
And naked sodden buttocks, mats of hair,
Bulged, clotted heads slept in the plastering slime.
And then the rain began, – the jolly old rain!

A yawning soldier knelt against the bank,
Staring across the morning blear with fog;
He wondered when the Allemands would get busy;
And then, of course, they started with five-nines
Traversing, sure as fate, and never a dud.
Mute in the clamour of shells he watched them burst
Spouting dark earth and wire with gusts from hell,
While posturing giants dissolved in drifts of smoke.
He crouched and flinched, dizzy with galloping fear,
Sick for escape, – loathing the strangled horror
And butchered, frantic gestures of the dead.

An officer came blundering down the trench:
'Stand-to and man the fire-step!' On he went . . .
Gasping and bawling, 'Fire-step . . . counter-attack!'
Then the haze lifted. Bombing on the right
Down the old sap: machine-guns on the left;
And stumbling figures looming out in front.
'O Christ, they're coming at us!' Bullets spat,
And he remembered his rifle . . . rapid fire . . .
And started blazing wildly . . . than a bang
Crumpled and spun him sideways, knocked him out
To grunt and wriggle: none heeded him; he choked
And fought the flapping veils of smothering gloom,
Lost in a blurred confusion of yells and groans . . .
Down, and down, and down, he sank and drowned,
Bleeding to death. The counter-attack had failed.

Written in July 1916

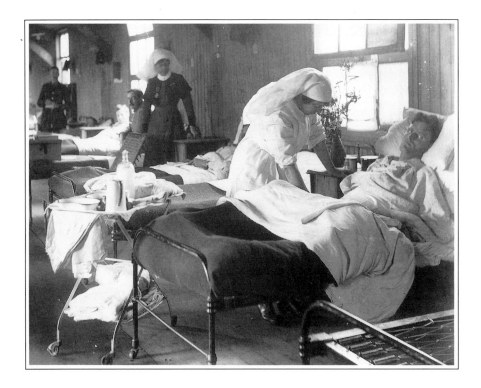

He drowsed and was aware of silence heaped
Round him, unshaken as the steadfast walls;
Aqueous like floating rays of amber light,
Soaring and quivering in the wings of sleep.
Silence and safety; and his mortal shore
Lipped by the inward, moonless waves of death.

Someone was holding water to his mouth.
He swallowed, unresisting; moaned and dropped
Through crimson gloom to darkness; and forgot
The opiate throb and ache that was his wound.
    Water – calm, sliding green above the weir.
    Water – a sky-lit alley for his boat,
    Bird-voiced, and bordered with reflected flowers
    And shaken hues of summer; drifting down,
    He dipped contented oars, and sighed, and slept.

Night, with a gust of wind, was in the ward,
Blowing the curtain to a glimmering curve.
Night. He was blind; he could not see the stars
Glinting among the wraiths of wandering cloud;
Queer blots of colour, purple, scarlet green,
Flickered and faded in his drowning eyes.

Rain – he could hear it rustling through the dark;
Fragrance and passionless music woven as one;
Warm rain on drooping roses; pattering showers
That soak the woods; not the harsh rain that sweeps
Behind the thunder, but a trickling peace,
Gently and slowly washing life away.

He stirred, shifting his body; then the pain
Leapt like a prowling beast, and gripped and tore
His groping dreams with grinding claws and fangs.
    But someone was beside him; soon he lay
    Shuddering because that evil thing had passed.
    And death, who'd stepped toward him, paused and stared.

Light many lamps and gather round his bed,
Lend him your eyes, warm blood, and will to live.
Speak to him; rouse him; you may save him yet.
He's young; he hated War; how should he die
When cruel old campaigners win safe through?

But death replied: 'I choose him.' So he went,
And there was silence in the summer night;
Silence and safety; and the veils of sleep.
Then, far away, the thudding of the guns.

Written in August 1916

WHO MADE THE LAW?   **Leslie Coulson**

Who made the Law that men should die in meadows?
Who spake the word that blood should splash in lanes?
Who gave it forth that gardens should be bone-yards?
Who spread the hills with flesh, and blood, and brains?
              Who made the Law?

Who made the Law that Death should stalk the village?
Who spake the word to kill among the sheaves,
Who gave it forth that death should lurk in hedgerows,
Who flung the dead among the fallen leaves?
              Who made the Law?

Those who return shall find that peace endures,
Find old things old, and know the things they knew,
Walk in the garden, slumber by the fireside,
Share the peace of dawn, and dream amid the dew –
                    Those who return.

Those who return shall till the ancient pastures,
Clean-hearted men shall guide the plough-horse reins,
Some shall grow apples and flowers in the valleys,
Some shall go courting in summer down the lanes –
                    THOSE WHO RETURN.

But who made the Law? the Trees shall whisper to him:
'See, see the blood – the splashes on our bark!'
Walking the meadows, he shall hear bones crackle,
And fleshless mouths shall gibber in silent lanes at dark.
                    Who made the Law?

Who made the Law? At noon upon the hillside
His ears shall hear a moan, his cheeks shall feel a breath,
And all along the valleys, past gardens, croft, and homesteads,
He who made the Law,
He who made the Law,
HE who made the Law shall walk alone with Death.
                    WHO made the Law?

Published in October 1916

THE DEAD FOXHUNTER   **Robert Graves**

We found the little captain at the head;
His men lay well aligned.
We touched his hand – stone cold – and he was dead,
And they, all dead behind,
Had never reached their goal, but they died well;
They charged in line, and in the same line fell.

The well-known rosy colours of his face
Were almost lost in grey,
We saw that, dying and in hopeless case,
For others' sake that day
He'd smothered all rebellious groans: in death
His fingers were tight clenched between his teeth.

For those who live uprightly and die true
Heaven has no bars or locks,
And serves all taste . . . or what's for him to do
Up there, but hunt the fox?
Angelic choirs? No, Justice must provide
For one who rode straight and in hunting died.

So if Heaven had no Hunt before he came,
Why, it must find one now:
If any shirk and doubt they know the game,
There's one to teach them how:
And the whole host of Seraphim complete
Must jog in scarlet to his opening Meet.

Written in memory of Captain Samson who was killed in September 1915.

FROM THE SOMME   **Leslie Coulson**

In other days I sang of simple things,
  Of summer dawn, and summer noon and night,
The dewy grass, the dew-wet fairy rings,
  The lark's long golden flight.

Deep in the forest I made melody
  While squirrels cracked their hazel nuts on high,
Or I would cross the wet sand to the sea
  And sing to sea and sky.

When came the silvered silence of the night
   I stole to casements over scented lawns,
And softly sang of love and love's delight
   To mute white marble fauns.

Oft in the tavern parlour I would sing
   Of morning sun upon the mountain vine,
And, calling for a chorus, sweep the string
   In praise of good red wine.

I played with all the toys the gods provide,
   I sang my songs and made glad holiday.
Now I have cast my broken toys aside
   And flung my lute away.

A singer once, I now am fain to weep.
   Within my soul I feel strange music swell,
Vast chants of tragedy too deep – too deep
   For my poor lips to tell.

Written in 1916

BALLAD OF THE THREE SPECTRES   Ivor Gurney

As I went up by Ovillers
   In mud and water cold to the knee,
There went three jeering, fleering spectres,
   That walked abreast and talked of me.

The first said, 'Here's a right brave soldier
   That walks the dark unfearingly;
Soon he'll come back on a fine stretcher,
   And laughing for a nice Blighty.'

The second, 'Read his face, old comrade,
    No kind of lucky chance I see;
One day he'll freeze in mud to the marrow,
    Then look his last on Picardie.'

Though bitter the word of these first twain
    Curses the third spat venomously;
'He'll stay untouched till the war's last dawning
    Then live one hour of agony.'

Liars the first two were. Behold me
    At sloping arms by one-two-three;
Waiting the time I shall discover
    Whether the third spake verity.

Written in February 1917

The House is crammed: tier beyond tier they grin
And cackle at the Show, while prancing ranks
Of harlots shrill the chorus, drunk with din;
'We're sure the Kaiser loves our dear old Tanks!'

I'd like to see a Tank come down the stalls,
Lurching to rag-time tunes, or 'Home, sweet Home',
And there'd be no more jokes in Music-halls
To mock the riddled corpses round Bapaume.

Written in February 1917

If I were fierce, and bald, and short of breath,
I'd live with scarlet Majors at the Base,
And speed glum heroes up the line to death.
You'd see me with my puffy petulant face,
Guzzling and gulping in the best hotel,
Reading the Roll of Honour. 'Poor young chap,'
I'd say – 'I used to know his father well;
Yes, we've lost heavily in this last scrap.'
And when the war is done and youth stone dead,
I'd toddle safely home and die – in bed.

Written in March 1917

From *DEAD MAN'S DUMP*   **Isaac Rosenberg**

The plunging limbers over the shattered track
Racketed with their rusty freight,
Stuck out like many crowns of thorns,
And the rusty stakes like sceptres old
To stay the flood of brutish men
Upon our brothers dear.

The wheels lurched over sprawled dead
But pained them not, though their bones crunched;
Their shut mouths made no moan.
They lie there huddled, friend and foeman,
Man born of man and born of woman;
And shells go crying over them
From night till night and now.

Earth has waited for them
All the time of their growth
Fretting for their decay:
Now she has them at last!
In the strength of their strength
Suspended – stopped and held.

What fierce imaginings their dark souls lit?
Earth! have they gone into you?
Somewhere they must have gone,
And flung on your hard back
Is their souls' sack,
Emptied of God-ancestralled essences.
Who hurled them out? Who hurled?

None saw their spirits' shadow shake the grass,
Or stood aside for the half used life to pass
Out of those doomed nostrils and the doomed mouth,
When the swift iron burning bee
Drained the wild honey of their youth.

What of us, who flung on the shrieking pyre,
Walk, our usual thoughts untouched,
Our lucky limbs as on ichor fed,
Immortal seeming ever?
Perhaps when the flames beat loud on us,
A fear may choke in our veins
And the startled blood may stop.

Written between February and May 1917

THE GENERAL   **Siegfried Sassoon**

'Good morning, good morning!' the General said
When we met him last week on our way to the line.
Now the soldiers he smiled at are most of 'em dead,
And we're cursing his staff for incompetent swine.
'He's a cheery old card', grunted Harry to Jack
As they slogged up to Arras with rifle and pack.

But he did for them both by his plan of attack.

Written in April 1917

Sixty years after the fall of Troy,
We, the old men – some of us nearly eighty-
Met and talked on the sunny rampart
Over our wine, while the lizards scuttled
In dusty grass, and the crickets chirred.

Some bared their wounds;
Some spoke of the thirst, dry in the throat,
And the heart-beat in the din of battle,
Some spoke of the intolerable sufferings
The brightness gone from their eyes
And the grey already thick in their hair.

And I sat a little apart
From their garrulous talk and old memories
And I heard a boy of twenty
Say petulantly to a girl, seizing her arm;

'Oh come away! Why do you stand there
Listening open mouthed to the talk of old men?
Haven't you heard enough of Troy and Achilles?
Why should they bore us for ever
With an old quarrel and the names of dead men
We never knew, and dull forgotten battles?'
And he drew her away,
And she looked back and laughed
As he spoke more contempt of us,
Being now out of hearing.

And I thought of all the graves by desolate Troy,
And the beauty of many young men now dust,
And the long agony, and how useless it all was.
And the talk still clashed about me
Like the meeting of blade and blade.
And as they two moved further away
He put an arm about her, and kissed her;
And afterwards I heard their gay distant laughter.

And I looked at the hollow cheeks
And the weary eyes and the grey streaked heads
Of the old men – nearly forty – about me;
And I too walked away
In an agony of helpless grief and pity.

Written in May 1917

The magpies in Picardy
Are more than I can tell.
They flicker down the dusty roads
And cast a magic spell
On the men who march through Picardy,
Through Picardy to hell.

(The blackbird flies with panic,
The swallow goes with light.
The finches move like ladies,
The owl floats by at night;
But the great and flashing magpie
He flies as artists might.)

A magpie in Picardy
Told me secret things –
Of the music in white feathers,
And the sunlight that sings
And dances in deep shadows –
He told me with his wings.

(The hawk is cruel and rigid,
He watches from a height;
The rook is slow and sombre,
The robin loves to fight;
But the great and flashing magpie
He flies as lovers might.)

He told me that in Picardy,
An age ago or more,
While all his fathers still were eggs,
These dusty highways bore
Brown, singing soldiers marching out
Through Picardy to war.

He said that still through chaos
Works on the ancient plan
And two things have altered not
Since first the world began –
The beauty of the wild green earth
And the bravery of man.

(For the sparrow flies unthinking
And quarrels in his flight;
The heron trails his legs behind,
The lark goes out of sight;
But the great and flashing magpie
He flies as poets might.)

Published in June 1917

It is midday; the deep trench glares . . .
A buzz and blaze of flies . . .
The hot wind puffs the giddy airs . . .
The great sun rakes the skies.

No sound in all the stagnant trench
Where forty standing men
Endure the sweat and grit and stench,
Like cattle in a pen.

Sometimes a sniper's bullet whirs
Or twangs the whining wire;
Sometimes a soldier sighs and stirs
As in Hell's frying fire.

From out a high cool cloud descends
An aeroplane's far moan . . .
The sun strikes down, the thin cloud rends
The black spot travels on.

And sweating, dizzied, isolate
In the hot trench beneath,
We bide the next shrewd move of fate
Be it of life or death.

Published in June 1917

Well, how are things in Heaven? I wish you'd say,
Because I'd like to know that you're all right.
Tell me, have you found everlasting day,
Or been sucked in by everlasting night?
For when I shut my eyes your face shows plain;
I hear you make some cheery old remark –
I can rebuild you in my brain,
Though you've gone out patrolling in the dark.

You hated tours of trenches; you were proud
Of nothing more than having good years to spend;
Longed to get home and join the careless crowd
Of chaps who work in peace with Time for friend.
That's all washed out now. You're beyond the wire:
No earthly chance can send you crawling back;
You've finished with machine-gun fire –
Knocked over in a hopeless dud-attack.

Somehow I always thought you'd get done in,
Because you were so desperate keen to live:
You were all out to try and save your skin,
Well knowing how much the world had got to give.
You joked at shells and talked the usual 'shop',
Stuck to your dirty job and did it fine;
With 'Jesus Christ! when will it stop?
Three years . . . It's hell unless we break their line'.

So when they told me you'd been left for dead
I wouldn't believe them, feeling it must be true.
Next week the bloody Roll of Honour said
'Wounded and missing' – (That's the thing to do
When lads are left in shell-holes dying slow,
With nothing but blank sky and wounds that ache,
Moaning for water till they know
It's night, and then it's not worthwhile to wake!)

Good-bye, old lad! Remember me to God,
And tell Him that our Politicians swear
They won't give in till Prussian Rule's been trod
Under the Heel of England . . . Are you there? . . .
Yes . . . and the War won't end for at least two years;
But we've got stacks of men . . . I'm blind with tears,
Staring into the dark. Cheero!
I wish they'd killed you in a decent show.

Written in June 1917

ANTHEM FOR DOOMED YOUTH   **Wilfred Owen**

What passing-bells for those who die as cattle?
Only the monstrous anger of the guns.
Only the stuttering rifles' rapid rattle
Can patter out their hasty orisons.
No mockeries for them from prayers or bells,
Nor any voice of mourning save the choirs, –
The shrill, demented choirs of wailing shells;
And bugles calling for them from sad shires.

What candles may be held to speed them all?
Not in the hands of boys, but in their eyes
Shall shine the holy glimmers of good-byes.
The pallor of girls' brows shall be their pall;
Their flowers the tenderness of patient minds,
And each slow dusk a drawing-down of blinds.

Written between September and October 1917

BEAUCOURT REVISITED   **A. P. Herbert**

I wandered up to Beaucourt; I took the river track,
And saw the lines we lived in before the Boche went back;
But Peace was now in Pottage, the front was far ahead,
The front had journeyed Eastward, and only left the dead.

And I thought, How long we lay there, and watched across the wire,
While the guns roared round the valley, and set the skies afire!
But now there are homes in Hamel and tents in the Vale of Hell,
And a camp at Suicide Corner where half a regiment fell.

The new troops follow after, and tread the land we won,
To them 'tis so much hillside re-wrested from the Hun;
We only walk with reverence this sullen mile of mud;
The shell holes hold our history, and half of them our blood.

Here, at the head of Peche Street, 'twas death to show your face;
To me it seemed like magic to linger in the place;
For me how many spirits hung round the Kentish Caves,
But the new men see no spirits – they only see the graves.

I found the half-dug ditches we fashioned for the fight
We lost a score of men there – young James was killed that night;
I saw the star shells staring, I heard the bullets hail,
But the new troops pass unheading – they never heard the tale.

I crossed the blood-red ribbon, that once was No Man's Land,
I saw a misty daybreak and a creeping minute-hand;
And here the lads went over, and there was Harmsworth shot,
And here was William lying – but the new men know them not.

And I said, 'There is still the river, and still the stiff, stark trees:
To treasure here our story, but there are only these';
But under the white wood crosses the dead men answered low,
'The new men know not Beaucourt, but we are here – we know'.

Published in September 1917

FIGHT TO A FINISH   **Siegfried Sassoon**

The boys came back. Bands played and flags were flying,
   And Yellow-Pressmen thronged the sunlit street
To cheer the soldiers who'd refrained from dying,
   And hear the music of returning feet.
'Of all the thrills and ardours War has brought,
This moment is the finest.' (So they thought.)

Snapping their bayonets on to charge the mob,
   Grim Fusiliers broke ranks with glint of steel,
At last the boys had found a cushy job.

   I heard the Yellow-Pressmen grunt and squeal;
And with my trusty bombers turned and went
To clear those Junkers out of Parliament.

Published in October 1917

DULCE ET DECORUM EST   **Wilfred Owen**

Bent double, like old beggars under sacks,
Knock-kneed, coughing like hags, we cursed through sludge,
Till on the haunting flares we turned our backs
And towards our distant rest began to trudge.
Men marched asleep. Many had lost their boots
But limped on, blood-shod. All went lame; all blind;
Drunk with fatigue; deaf even to the hoots
Of gas-shells dropping softly behind.

Gas! GAS! Quick, boys! – An ecstasy of fumbling,
Fitting the clumsy helmets just in time;
But someone still was yelling out and stumbling
And flound'ring like a man in fire or lime . . .
Dim, through the misty panes and thick green light,
As under a green sea, I saw him drowning.

In all my dreams, before my helpless sight,
He plunges at me, guttering, choking, drowning.

If in some smothering dreams you too could pace
Behind the wagon that we flung him in,
And watch the white eyes writhing in his face,
His hanging face, like a devil's sick of sin;
If you could hear, at every jolt, the blood
Come gargling from the froth-corrupted lungs,
Obscene as cancer, bitter as the cud
Of vile, incurable sores on innocent tongues, –
My friend, you would not tell with such high zest
To children ardent for some desperate glory,
The old Lie: Dulce et decorum est
Pro patria mori.

Drafted in October 1917, and later revised in early 1918.

DOES IT MATTER?   **Siegfried Sassoon**

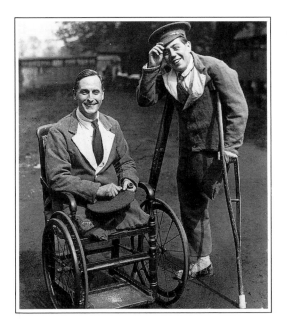

Does it matter? – losing your legs? . . .
For people will always be kind,
And you need not show that you mind
When the others come in after hunting
To gobble their muffins and eggs.

Does it matter? – losing your sight? . . .
There's such splendid work for the blind;
And people will always be kind,
As you sit on the terrace remembering
And turning your face to the light.

Do they matter? – those dreams from the pit? . . .
You can drink and forget and be glad,
And people won't say that you're mad;
For they'll know that you've fought for your country
And no one will worry a bit.

Published in October 1917

ATTACK   **Siegfried Sassoon**

At dawn the ridge emerges massed and dun
In the wild purple of the glow'ring sun,
Smouldering through spouts of drifting smoke that shroud
The menacing scarred slope; and, one by one,
Tanks creep and topple forward to the wire.
The barrage roars and lifts. Then, clumsily bowed
With bombs and guns and shovels and battle-gear,
Men jostle and climb to meet the bristling fire.
Lines of grey, muttering faces, masked with fear,
They leave their trenches, going over the top,
While time ticks blank and busy on their wrists,
And hope, with furtive eyes and grappling fists,
Flounders in mud. O Jesus, make it stop!

Published in October 1917

I, too, saw God through mud, –
The mud that cracked on cheeks when wretches smiled.
War brought more glory to their eyes than blood,
And gave their laughs more glee than shakes a child.

Merry it was to laugh there –
Where death becomes absurd and life absurder.
For power was on us as we slashed bones bare
Not to feel sickness or remorse of murder.

I, too, have dropped off Fear –
Behind the barrage, dead as my platoon,
And sailed my spirit surging light and clear
Past the entanglement where hopes lay strewn;

And witnessed exultation –
Faces that used to curse me, scowl for scowl,
Shine and lift up with passion of oblation,
Seraphic for an hour; though they were foul.

I have made fellowships –
Untold of happy lovers in old song.
For love is not the binding of fair lips
With the soft silk of eyes that look and long,

By Joy, whose ribbon slips, –
But wound with war's hard wire whose stakes are strong;
Bound with the bandage of the arm that drips;
Knit in the webbing of the rifle-thong.

I have perceived much beauty
In the hoarse oaths that kept our courage straight;
Heard music in the silentness of duty;
Found peace where shell-storms spouted reddest spate.

Nevertheless, except you share
With them in hell the sorrowful dark of hell,
Whose world is but the trembling of a flare
And heaven but as the highway for a shell.

You shall not hear their mirth:
You shall not come to think them well content
By any jest of mine. These men are worth
Your tears. You are not worth their merriment.

Written between November and December 1917

You love us when we're heroes, home on leave,
Or wounded in a mentionable place,
You worship decorations; you believe
That chivalry redeems the war's disgrace.
You make us shells. You listen with delight,
By tales of dirt and danger fondly thrilled.

You crown our distant ardours while we fight,
And mourn our laurelled memories when we're killed.
You can't believe that British troops 'retire'
When hell's last horror breaks them, and they run,
Trampling the terrible corpses – blind with blood.
O German mother dreaming by the fire,
While you are knitting socks to send your son
His face is trodden deeper in the mud.

Published in December 1917

THE DESERTER   **Gilbert Frankau**

'I'm sorry I done it, Major.'
We bandaged the livid face;
And led him out, ere the wan sun rose,
To die his death of disgrace.

The bolt-heads locked to the cartridge;
The rifles steadied to rest,
As cold stock nestled at colder cheek
And foresight lined on the breast.

'Fire!' called the Sergeant-Major.
The muzzles flamed as he spoke:
And the shameless soul of a nameless man
Went up in the cordite-smoke.

Written in 1917

HERE DEAD LIE WE   **A. E. Housman**

Here dead lie we because we did not choose
To live and shame the land from which we sprung.
Life, to be sure, is nothing much to lose;
But young men think it is, and we were young.

Published in 1917

FIELD MANOEUVRES   Richard Aldington

The long autumn grass under my body
Soaks my clothes with its dew;
Where my knees press into the ground
I can feel the damp earth.

In my nostrils is the smell of the crushed grass,
Wet pine-cones and bark.

Through the great bronze pine trunks
Glitters a silver segment of road.
Interminable squadrons of silver and blue horses
Pace in long ranks the blank fields of heaven.

There is no sound;
The wind hisses gently through the pine needles;

The flutter of a finch's wings about my head
Is like distant thunder,
And the shrill cry of a mosquito
Sounds loud and close.

I am 'to fire at the enemy column
After it has passed' –
But my obsolete rifle, loaded with 'blank',
Lies untouched before me,
My spirit follows after the gliding clouds,
And my lips murmur of the mother beauty
Standing breast-high, in golden broom
Among the blue pine-woods!

Published in 1917

Robert Graves

Yet once an earlier David took
Smooth pebbles from the brook:
Out between the lines he went
To that one-sided tournament,
A shepherd boy who stood out fine
And young to fight a Philistine
Clad all in brazen mail. He swears
That he's killed lions, he's killed bears,
And those that scorn the God of Zion
Shall perish so like bear or lion.
But . . . the historian of that fight
Had not the heart to tell it right.

Striding within javelin range,
Goliath marvels at this strange
Goodly-faced boy so proud of strength.
David's clear eye measures the length;
With hand thrust back, he cramps one knee,
Poises a moment thoughtfully,
And hurls with a long vengeful swing.
The pebble, humming from the sling
Like a wild bee, flies a sure line
For the forehead of the Philistine;
Then ... but there comes a brazen clink,
And quicker than a man can think
Goliath's shield parries each cast.
Clang! clang! and clang! was David's last.
Scorn blazes in the Giant's eye,
Towering unhurt six cubits high.

Says foolish David, 'Damn your shield!
And damn my sling! but I'll not yield.'
He takes his staff of Mamre oak,
A knotted shepherd-staff that's broke
The skull of many a wolf and fox
Come filching lambs from Jesse's flocks.
Loud laughs Goliath, and that laugh
Can scatter chariots like blown chaff
To rout; but David, calm and brave,
Holds his ground, for God will save.

Steel crosses wood, a flash, and oh!
Shame for beauty's overthrow!
(God's eyes are dim, His ears are shut.)
One cruel backhand sabre-cut –
'I'm hit! I'm killed!' young David cries,
Throws blindly forward, chokes ... and dies.
And look, spike-helmeted, grey, grim,
Goliath straddles over him.

Published in 1917

TWO FUSILIERS   **Robert Graves**

And have we done with War at last?
Well, we've been lucky devils both,
And there's no need of pledge or oath
To bind our lovely friendship fast,
By firmer stuff
Close bound enough.

By wire and wood and stake we're bound,
By Fricourt and Festubert,
By whipping rain, by the sun's glare,
By all the misery and loud sound,
By a Spring day,
By Picard clay.

Show me the two so closely bound
As we, by the wet bond of blood,
By friendship blossoming from mud,
By Death: we faced him, and we found
Beauty in Death,
In dead men, breath.

Published in 1917

SPORTSMEN IN PARADISE T. P. Cameron Wilson

They left the fury of the fight,
And they were very tired.
The gates of Heaven were open, quite
Unguarded, and unwired.
There was no sound of any gun:
The land was still and green:
Wide hills lay silent in the sun,
Blue valleys slept between.

They saw far off a little wood
Stand up against the sky.
Knee deep in grass a great tree stood . . .
Some lazy cows went by . . .
There were some rooks sailed overhead –
And once a church-bell pealed.
'God! but it's England', someone said,
'And there's a cricket field!'

Published in 1917

Same old trenches, same old view,
Same old rats as blooming tame,
Same old dug-outs, nothing new,
Same old smell, the very same,
Same old bodies out in front,
Same old strafe from two till four,
Same old scratching, same old 'unt,
Same old bloody war.

Published in March 1917

HIGH WOOD   Philip Johnstone

Ladies and gentlemen, this is High Wood,
Called by the French, Bois des Fourneaux,
The famous spot which in Nineteen-Sixteen,
July, August and September was the scene
Of long and bitterly contested strife,
By reason of its High commanding site.
Observe the effect of shell-fire in the trees
Standing and fallen; here is wire; this trench
For months inhabited, twelve times changed hands;
(They soon fall in), used later as a grave.
It has been said on good authority
That in the fighting for this patch of wood
Were killed somewhere above eight thousand men,
Of whom the greater part were buried here,
This mound on which you stand being . . .

Madame, please,
You are requested kindly not to touch
Or take away the Company's property
As souvenirs. your'll find we have on sale
A large variety, all guaranteed.
As I was saying, all is as it was,
This is an unknown British officer,
The tunic having lately rotted off.
Please follow me – this way . . .
                    the path, sir, please,

The ground which was secured at great expense
The Company keeps absolutely untouched,
And in that dug-out (genuine) we provide
Refreshments at a reasonable rate.
You are requested not to leave about
Paper, or ginger-beer bottles, or orange-peel,
There are waste-paper baskets at the gate.

Published in February 1918

SUICIDE IN THE TRENCHES   **Siegfried Sassoon**

I knew a simple soldier boy
Who grinned at life in empty joy,
Slept soundly through the lonesome dark,
And whistled early with the lark.

In winter trenches, cowed and glum,
With crumps and lice and lack of rum,
He put a bullet through his brain.
No one spoke of him again.

You smug-faced crowds with kindling eye
Who cheer when soldier lads march by,
Sneak home and pray you'll never know
The hell where youth and laughter go.

Published in February 1918

STRANGE MEETING   **Wilfred Owen**

It seemed that out of battle I escaped
Down some profound dull tunnel, long since scooped
Through granites which titanic wars had groined.

Yet also there encumbered sleepers groaned,
Too fast in thought or death to be bestirred.
Then, as I probed them, one sprang up, and started
With piteous recognition in fixed eyes,
Lifting distressful hands as if to bless.
And by his smile, I knew that sullen hall,
By his dead smile I knew we stood in Hell.

With a thousand pains that vision's face was grained;
Yet no blood reached there from the upper ground,
And no guns thumped, or down the flues made moan.
'Strange friend,' I said, 'here is no cause to mourn.'
'None,' said the other, 'save the undone years,
The hopelessness. Whatever hope is yours,
Was my life also; I went hunting wild
After the wildest beauty in the world,
Which lies not in calm eyes, or braided hair,
But mocks the steady running of the hour,
And if it grieves, grieves richlier than here.
For of my glee might many men have laughed,
And of my weeping something had been left,
Which must die now. I mean the truth untold,
The pity of war, the pity war distilled.
Now men will go content with what we spoiled,
Or discontent, boil bloody, and be spilled.
They will be swift with swiftness of the tigress.
None will break ranks, though nations trek from progress.

Courage was mine, and I had mystery,
Wisdom was mine, and I had mastery:
To miss the march of this retreating world
Into vain citadels that are not walled.
Then, when much blood had clogged their chariot-wheels,
I would go up and wash them from sweet wells,
Even with truths that lie too deep for taint.
I would have poured my spirit without stint
But not through wounds; not on the cess of war.
Foreheads of men have bled where no wounds were.

I am the enemy you killed, my friend.
I knew you in this dark: for so you frowned
Yesterday through me as you jabbed and killed.
I parried; but my hands were loath and cold.
Let us sleep now . . .'

Written in March 1918

IN THE GALLERY WHERE THE FAT MEN GO

Louis Golding

They are showing how we lie
With our bodies run dry:
The attitudes we take
When impaled upon a stake.
These and other things they show
In the gallery where the fat men go.

In the gallery where the fat men go
They're exhibiting our guts
Horse-betrampled in the ruts;
And Private Tommy Spout,
With one eye gouged out;
And Jimmy spitting blood;
And Sergeant lying so
That he's drowning in the mud,
In the gallery where the fat men go.

They adjust their pince-nez
In the gentle urban way,
And they plant their feet tight
For to get a clearer sight
They stand playing with their thumbs,
With their shaven cheeks aglow,
For the terror never comes,
And the worms and the woe.
For they never hear the drums
Drumming Death dead-slow,
In the gallery where the fat men go.

If the gallery where the fat men go
Were in flames around their feet,
Or were sucking through the mud:
If they heard the guns beat
Like a pulse through the blood:
If the lice were in their hair,
And the scabs were on their tongue,
And the rats were smiling there,
Padding softly through the dung,
Would they fix the pince-nez
In the gentle urban way,
Would the pictures still be hung
In the gallery where the fat men go?

Published in May 1918

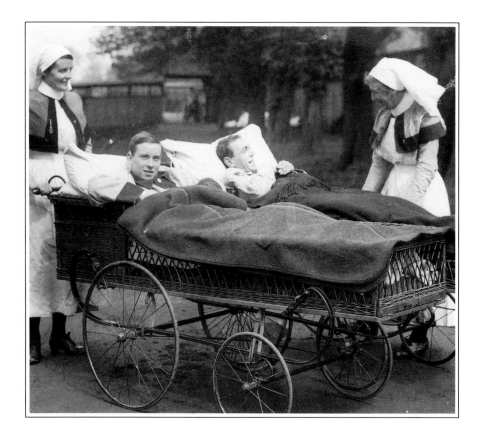

He sat in a wheeled chair, waiting for dark,
And shivered in his ghastly suit of grey,
Legless, sewn short at elbow. Through the park
Voices of boys rang saddening like a hymn,
Voices of play and pleasure after day,
Till gathering sleep had mothered them from him.

About this time Town used to swing so gay
When glow-lamps budded in the light blue trees,
And girls glanced lovelier as the air grew dim, –
In the old times, before he threw away his knees.
Now he will never feel again how slim
Girls' waists are, or how warm their subtle hands;
All of them touch him like some queer disease.

There was an artist silly for his face,
For it was younger than his youth, last year.
Now, he is old; his back will never brace;
He's lost his colour very far from here,
Poured it down shell-holes till the veins ran dry,
And half his lifetime lapsed in the hot race,
And leap of purple spurted from his thigh.

One time he liked a blood-smear down his leg,
After the matches, carried shoulder-high.
It was after football, when he'd drunk a peg,
He thought he'd better join. – He wonders why.
Someone had said he'd look a god in kilts,
That's why; and maybe, too, to please his Meg;
Aye, that was it, to please the giddy jilts
He asked to join. He didn't have to beg;
Smiling they wrote his lie; aged nineteen years.
Germans he scarcely thought of; all their guilt,
And Austria's, did not move him. And no fears
Of Fear came yet. He thought of jewelled hilts
For daggers in plaid socks; of smart salutes;
And care of arms; and leave; and pay arrears;
Esprit de corps; and hints for young recruits.
And soon, he was drafted out with drums and cheers.

Some cheered him home, but not as crowds cheer Goal.
Only a solemn man who brought him fruits
Thanked him; and then inquired about his soul.

Now, he will spend a few sick years in Institutes,
And do what things the rules consider wise,
And take whatever pity they may dole,
To-night he noticed how the women's eyes
Passed from him to the strong men that were whole.
How cold and late it is! Why don't they come
And put him into bed? Why don't they come?

Completed in July 1918

THE DUG OUT   **Siegfried Sassoon**

Why do you lie with your legs ungainly huddled,
And one arm bent across your sullen, cold,
Exhausted face? It hurts my heart to watch you,
Deep-shadow'd from the candle's guttering gold;
And you wonder why I shake you by the shoulder;
Drowsy, you mumble and sigh and turn your head ...
You are too young to fall asleep for ever;
And when you sleep you remind me of the dead.

Written in July 1918

THE PARABLE OF THE OLD MEN AND THE YOUNG   **Wilfred Owen**

So Abram rose, and clave the wood, and went,
And took the fire with him, and a knife.
And as they sojourned both of them together,
Isaac the first-born spake and said, My Father,
Behold the preparations, fire and iron,
But where the lamb for this burnt offering?
Then Abram bound the youth with belts and straps,
And builded parapets and trenches there,
And stretchèd forth the knife to slay his son.
When lo! an angel called him out of heaven,
Saying, Lay not thy hand upon the lad,
Neither do anything to him. Behold,
A ram, caught in a thicket by its horns;
Offer the Ram of Pride instead of him.
But the old man would not so, but slew his son,
And half the seed of Europe, one by one.

Written in July 1918

EXPOSURE   **Wilfred Owen**

Our brains ache, in the merciless iced east winds that knive us . . .
Wearied we keep awake because the night is silent . . .
Low, drooping flares confuse our memory of the salient . . .
Worried by silence, sentries whisper, curious, nervous,
But nothing happens.

Watching, we hear the mad gusts tugging on the wire,
Like twitching agonies of men among its brambles.
Northward, incessantly, the flickering gunnery rumbles,
Far'off, like a dull rumour of some other war.
What are we doing here?

The poignant misery of dawn begins to grow . . .
We only know war lasts, rain soaks, and clouds sag stormy.
Dawn massing in the east her melancholy army
Attacks once more in ranks on shivering ranks of gray,
But nothing happens.

Sudden successive flights of bullets streak the silence.
Less deathly than the air that shudders black with snow,
With sidelong flowing flakes that flock, pause, and renew;
We watch them wandering up and down the wind's nonchalance,
But nothing happens.

Pale flakes with fingering stealth come feeling for our faces –
We cringe in holes, back on forgotten dreams, and stare, snow-dazed,
Deep into grassier ditches. So we drowse, sun-dozed,
Littered with blossoms trickling where the blackbird fusses.
Is it that we are dying?

Slowly our ghosts drag home: glimpsing the sunk fires, glozed
With crusted dark-red jewels; crickets jingle there;
For hours the innocent mice rejoice: the house is theirs;
Shutters and doors, all closed: on us the doors are closed, –
We turn back to our dying.

Since we believe not otherwise can kind fires burn;
Nor ever suns smile true on child, or field, or fruit.
For God's invincible spring our love is made afraid;
Therefore, not loath, we lie out here; therefore were born,
For love of God seems dying.

Tonight, this frost will fasten on this mud and us,
Shrivelling many hands, puckering foreheads crisp.
The burying-party, picks and shovels in their shaking grasp,
Pause over half-known faces. All their eyes are ice,
But nothing happens.

Completed in September 1918

So they are satisfied with our Brigade,
And it remains to parcel out the bays!
And we shall have the usual Thanks Parade,
The beaming General, and the soapy praise.

You will come up in your capricious car
To find your heroes sulking in the rain,
To tell us how magnificent we are,
And how you hope we'll do the same again.

And we, who knew your old abusive tongue,
Who heard you hector us a week before,
We who have bled to boost you up a rung –
A K.C.B. perhaps, perhaps a Corps –

We who must mourn those spaces in the mess,
And somehow fill those hollows in the heart,
We do not want your Sermon on Success,
Your greasy benisons on Being Smart.

We only want to take our wounds away.
To some warm village where the tumult ends,
And drowsing in the sunshine many a day,
Forget our aches, forget that we had friends.

Weary we are of blood and noise and pain;
This was a week we shall not soon forget;
And if, indeed, we have to fight again,
We little wish to think about it yet.

We have done well; we like to hear it said.
Say it, and then, for God's sake, say no more.
Fight, if you must, fresh battles far ahead,
But keep them dark behind your chateau door!

Published in 1918

OUTPOSTS   **F. W. D. Bendall**

Sentry, sentry, what did you see
At gaze from your post beside Lone Tree?
A star-shell flared like a burning brand
But I saw no movement in No Man's Land.

Sentry, sentry what did you hear
As the night-wind fluttered the grasses near?
I heard a rifle-shot on the flank,
And my mate slid down to the foot of the bank.

Sentry, sentry, what did you do,
And hadn't your mate a word for you?
I lifted his head and called his name.
His lips moved once, but no sound came.

Sentry, sentry, what did you say
As you watched alone till break of day?
I prayed the Lord that I'd fire straight
If I saw the man that killed my mate.

Published in 1918

WINTER WARFARE   E. Rickword

Colonel Cold strode up the Line
(Tabs of rime and spurs of ice),
Stiffened all where he did glare,
Horses, men, and lice.

Visited a forward post,
Left them burning, ear to foot;
Fingers stuck to biting steel,
Toes to frozen boot.

Stalked on into No Man's Land,
Turned the wire to fleecy wool,
Iron stakes to sugar sticks
Snapping at a pull.

Those who watched with hoary eyes
Saw two figures gleaming there;
Hauptman Kälte, Colonel Cold,
Gaunt, in the grey air.

Stiffly, tinkling spurs they moved
Glassy eyed, with glinting heel
Stabbing those who lingered there
Torn by screaming steel.

Written after 1918

THE TARGET   **Ivor Gurney**

I shot him, and it had to be
One of us! 'Twas him or me.
'Couldn't be helped,' and none can blame
Me, for you would do the same.

My mother, she can't sleep for fear
Of what might be a-happening here
To me. Perhaps it might be best
To die, and set her fears at rest.

For worst is worst, and worry's done.
Perhaps he was the only son ...
Yet God keeps still, and does not say
A word of guidance any way.

Well, if they get me, first I'll find
That boy, and tell him all my mind,
And see who felt the bullet worst,
And ask his pardon, if I durst.

All's tangle, Here's my job.
A man might rave, or shout, or sob;
And God He takes no sort of heed.
This is a bloody mess indeed.

Published in 1919

I could not dig; I dared not rob:
Therefore I lied to please the mob.
Now all my lies are proved untrue
And I must face the men I slew.
What tale shall serve me here among
Mine angry and defrauded young?

Published in 1919

SOLILOQUY 2   **Richard Aldington**

I was wrong, quite wrong!
The dead men are not always carrion.
After the advance,
As we went through the shattered trenches
Which the enemy had left,
We found, lying upon the fire-step,
A dead English soldier,
His head bloodily bandaged
And his closed left hand touching the earth,

More beautiful than one can tell,
More subtly coloured than a perfect Goya,
And more austere and lovely in repose
Than Angelo's hand could ever carve in stone.

Published in 1919

MY MEN GO WEARILY **Herbert Read**

My men go wearily
With their monstrous burdens.

They bear wooden planks
And iron sheeting
Through the area of death.

When a flare curves through the sky
They rest immobile.

Then on again,
Sweating and blaspheming –
'Oh, bloody Christ!'

My men, my modern Christs,
Your bloody agony confronts the world.

Published in 1919

GETHSEMANE 1914–18   **Rudyard Kipling**

The Garden called Gethsemane,
In Picardy it was,
And there the people came to see
The English soldiers pass.
We used to pass – we used to pass
Or halt, as it might be,
And ship our masks in case of gas
Beyond Gethsemane.

The Garden called Gethsemane,
It held a pretty lass,
But all the time she talked to me
I prayed my cup might pass.
The officer sat on the chair,
The men lay on the grass,
And all the time we halted there
I prayed my cup might pass.

It didn't pass – it didn't pass –
It didn't pass from me.
I drank it when we met the gas
Beyond Gethsemane!

Published in 1919

Have you forgotten yet? ...
For the world's events have rumbled on since those gagged days,
Like traffic checked while at the crossing of city-ways:
And the haunted gap in your mind has filled with thoughts that flow
Like clouds in the lit heavens of life; and you're a man reprieved to go,
Taking your peaceful share of Time, with joy to spare.
But the past is just the same – and War's a bloody game ...
Have you forgotten yet? ...
Look down, and swear by the slain of the War that you'll never forget.

Do you remember the dark months you held the sector at Mametz –
The nights you watched and wired and dug and piled sandbags on parapets?
Do you remember the rats; and the stench
Of corpses rotting in front of the front-line trench –
And dawn coming, dirty-white, and chill with a hopeless rain?
Do you ever stop and ask, 'Is it all going to happen again?'

Do you remember that hour of din before the attack –
And the anger, the blind compassion that seized and shook you then
As you peered at the doomed and haggard faces of your men?
Do you remember the stretcher-cases lurching back
With dying eyes and lolling heads – those ashen-grey
Masks of the lads who once were keen and kind and gay?

Have you forgotten yet?
Look up, and swear by the green of the spring that you'll never forget.

Published in March 1919

THE CONSCRIPT   W. W. Gibson

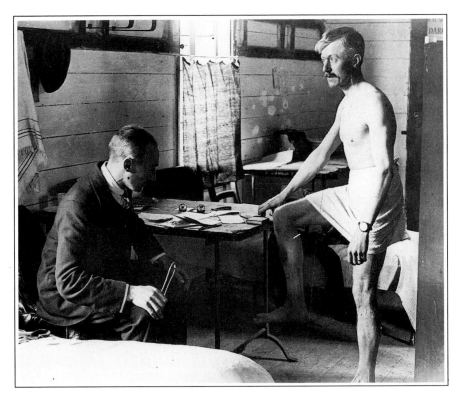

Indifferent, flippant, earnest, but all bored,
The doctors sit in the glare of electric light
Watching the endless stream of naked white
Bodies of men for whom their hasty award
Means life or death maybe, or the living death
Of mangled limbs, blind eyes, or a darkened brain;
And the chairman, as his monocle falls again,
Pronounces each doom with easy indifferent breath.

Then suddenly I shudder as I see
A young man stand before them wearily,
Cadaverous as one already dead;
But still they stare untroubled as he stands
With arms outstretched and drooping thorn-crowned head,
The nail-marks glowing in his feet and hands.

Published in 1920

ELEGY IN A COUNTRY CHURCHYARD

G. K. Chesterton

The men that worked for England
They have their graves at home:
And bees and birds of England
About the cross can roam.

But they that fought for England,
Following a falling star,
Alas, alas for England
They have their graves afar.

And they that rule in England,
In stately conclave met,
Alas, alas for England
They have no graves as yet.

Published in 1922

BARBED WIRE   **R. H. Sauter**

What bramble thicket this – grown overnight
on the clean earth – unflowering? In the dusk,
some mad end, loosened, taps upon its pole:
thorns tapping like the ghosts of dead delight.

Wire, barbed wire! – A dour
and monstrous serpent round our lives,
and we're like creatures mesmerized;
it glares at us, all day, malignant, sour,

Wire – fifteen feet of crouching coils-to lock
man out from Heaven's wonder!
And yet, each evening, grey moths come to mock
and conjure it asunder.

A No Man's Land, where little things can creep
and love and dance together;
flowers live ensanctuaried and crickets 'cheep';
birds sing in silent weather.

Wire – in Winter-time the snow
comes writhing down to perch on it
in great festoons. White-tented, now,
the distance marches in a bit.

Published in 1922

THE WATCHERS   **Edmund Blunden**

I heard the Challenge 'Who goes there?'
Close-kept but mine through midnight air;
I answered and was recognized,
And passed, and kindly thus advised:
'There's someone crawlin' through the grass
By the red ruin, or there was,
And them machine-guns been a firin'
All the time the chaps was wirin',
So sir if you're goin' out
You'll keep your 'ead well down no doubt.'

When will the stern fine 'Who goes there?'
Meet me again in midnight air?
And the gruff sentry's kindness, when
Will kindness have such power again?
It seems, as now I wake and brood,
And know my hour's decrepitude,
That on some dewy parapet
The sentry's spirit gazes yet,
Who will not speak with altered tone
When I at last am seen and known.

Published in 1928

CONCERT PARTY: BUSSEBOOM Edmund Blunden

The stage was set, the house was packed,
The famous troop began;
Our laughter thundered, act by act;
Time light as sunbeams ran.

Dance sprang and spun and neared and fled,
Jest chirped at gayest pitch,
Rhythm dazzled, action sped
Most comically rich.

With generals and lame privates both
Such charms worked wonders, till
The show was over; lagging loth
We faced the sunset chill.

And standing on the sandy way,
With the cracked church peering past,
We heard another matinée
We heard the maniac blast

Of barrage south by Saint Eloi,
And the red lights flaming there
Called madness: Come, my bonny boy,
And dance to the lastest air.

To this new concert, white we stood;
Cold certainty held our breath;
While men in the tunnels below Larch Wood
Were kicking men to death.

Published in 1928

BIOGRAPHIES

Richard Aldington
(1892–1962)
Educated at Dover College and London University. He volunteered in 1914, but was rejected on medical grounds. He was able to enlist in 1916, joining the Royal Sussex Regiment as a private. In 1918 he was invalided out (as a lieutenant) suffering from shell shock and the effects of gas.

After the war he wrote *Death of a Hero* and several biographies.

F. W. Bendall (1882–1953)
Awarded a classical scholarship to Cambridge, then joined the army. By 1914 he was a lieutenant colonel in the London Regiment, and later saw action at Gallipoli and in France, where he was wounded.

From 1940 to 1942 he was director of army education.

Laurence Binyon
(1869–1943)
Educated at St. Paul's and Trinity College, Oxford. He worked in the Department of Oriental Prints and Drawings at the British Museum, and then went to the Front as a Red Cross orderly in 1916.

Professor of Poetry at Harvard University in later life.

Edmund Blunden
(1896–1974)
Educated at Christ's Hospital and awarded a scholarship to Oxford in 1914, but enlisted instead. As an officer in the Royal Sussex Regiment, he experienced some of the bloodiest fighting on the Western Front, taking part in the later Somme battles (1916) and Passchendaele (1917). He was awarded the Military Cross and then had to be invalided out of the army in March 1918.

In 1928 he published an outstanding account of his experiences in *Undertones of War*. Between the wars he held posts at Tokyo and Oxford Universities.

Rupert Brooke (1887–1915)
Educated at Rugby and King's College, Cambridge. In 1914 he was given a commission in the Royal Naval Division by Winston Churchill, and then saw action in the retreat from Antwerp. His five famous war sonnets were written on leave after this campaign.

On the way to the Gallipoli campaign he suffered from acute blood poisoning, dying on St. George's Day. He was buried by a small group of friends on the Greek island of Skyros.

David Westcott Brown
(1892–1916)
Educated at the Dragon School, Marlborough and Balliol College, Oxford. He was commissioned in August 1914 in the Leicester Regiment, and was killed on 14 July 1916 at Bazentin le Petit during the Battle of the Somme.

G. K. Chesterton
(1874–1936)
A poet and successful novelist who took the side of the ordinary man against capitalism and socialism. He was strongly opposed to most of the press and to international

finance. He was a large man with a great sense of humour.

Leslie Coulson (1889–1916)

Recognized as one of the more brilliant young journalists before the war. He enlisted in the Royal Fusiliers, preferring to stay in the ranks rather than take a commission. He served in Egypt, was wounded at Gallipoli and was killed on 1 July 1916 during the opening moments of the Somme attack.

Gilbert Frankau (1884–1952)

Educated at Eton, and then travelled the world before the war. He was commissioned into the East Surrey Regiment in 1914, then transferred to the Royal Artillery in 1915. He fought at Loos, Ypres and the Somme, then was invalided out with shell shock in February 1918.

During the Second World War he was a squadron leader in the R.A.F.

W. W. Gibson (1878–1962)

Born in Hexham, Northumberland, he had no formal education. He worked as a social worker in the East End of London. He was a close friend of Rupert Brooke and tried to dissuade Brooke from enlisting.

Despite failing the medical, he persisted and served in the Royal Army Service Corps, but was never in the front line.

Louis Golding (1895–1958)

Educated at Manchester Grammar School and Oxford University after the war. He did not pass the army medical, so worked in an ambulance unit in Salonica and France.

Robert Graves (1895–1986)

Educated at Charterhouse and St. John's College, Oxford, after the war. He was commissioned in the Royal Welch Fusiliers where he formed a firm friendship with Siegfried Sassoon. He saw action at the Battle of Loos (1915) and at the Somme (1916), where he was critically wounded, his 'death' being announced in *The Times*.

After the war he enhanced his literary reputation by writing such books as *Goodbye to All That* (in just a few weeks) and *I Claudius*.

He was Professor of Poetry at Oxford University from 1961 to 1966, and then spent most of his final years living on the island of Majorca.

Julian Grenfell (1888–1915)

Educated at Eton and Balliol College, Oxford. He was commissioned into the Royal Dragoons in 1910, seeing service in India and South Africa. He enjoyed the precarious existence of life in the trenches and was awarded the D.S.O. for his bravery in the front lines.

After leave in January 1915, Grenfell returned to France with his three greyhounds. On 13 May he was struck by a shell splinter, and as he lay bleeding said to a senior officer, 'Don't bother about me, I'm done.' His friends believed that his toughness would pull him through, but he died on 26 May.

Ivor Gurney (1890–1937)

Educated at King's School, Gloucester and the Royal College of Music. He enlisted as a private in the Gloucester Regiment in 1915 and served on the Western Front from May 1916 until he was gassed in September 1917.

There had been signs of mental disorder before the war, but they now became more pronounced and he was forced to spend the rest of his life in a psychiatric hospital.

Thomas Hardy (1840–1928)

Born in Bockhampton in Dorset, the son of a stonemason. He started his working life as an architect, but then turned to writing. His famous novels about Wessex were published between 1871 and 1896. He was regarded at the time by many younger literary figures such as Sassoon as the greatest living English poet.

A. P. Herbert (1890–1971)

Educated at Winchester and New College, Oxford. He served with the Royal Naval Division at Gallipoli in 1915 and then on the Somme (1916). In April 1917 he was severely wounded and invalided out. After the war he became famous for his wit and humour and served as Independent MP for Oxford University from 1935 to 1950.

W. N. Hodgson (1893–1916)

Youngest son of the Bishop of St. Edmundsbury and Ipswich, he was educated at Durham School where he was an outstanding sportsman. He gained a First in Classics at Christ Church College, Oxford, and was commissioned into the 9th Devonshire Regiment in 1914. He was mentioned in despatches and awarded the Military Cross in 1915. On 1 July 1916 (the first day of the Somme) he was killed as the Devonshire Regiment attacked the fortified village of Mametz.

A. E. Housman (1859–1936)

A brilliant scholar who failed his finals at Oxford and then became Professor of Latin at London University, and later, Cambridge.

His collection of poetry *A Shropshire Lad* (1896) had a profound influence on many of the war poets.

Philip Johnstone

No information is available

Rudyard Kipling (1865–1936)

A prolific writer of poetry and novels throughout his life. He was one of the few who had written about the ordinary soldier before the war. His only son, a lieutenant in the Irish Guards, was killed at the Battle of Loos in 1915. Consequently, much of Kipling's poetry became bitter. He is responsible for the standard inscription to be found in war cemeteries: 'Their names liveth for evermore'.

W. S. Lyon (1886–1915)

Educated at Haileybury and Oxford, he joined the Royal Scots before the war and was a lieutenant in 1913. He saw service in France and Belgium and was killed near Ypres on 8 May 1915.

John McCrae (1872–1918)

A Canadian doctor who joined the army as a gunner, then transferred to the medical service. In January 1918 he was made consultant to all the British armies in France, but died of pneumonia before taking up his appointment.

A. A. Milne (1882–1956)

Educated at Westminster and Trinity College, Cambridge. He was commissioned in the Royal Warwickshire Regiment and fought in the Battle of the Somme. Some of his poems were published in *Punch*.

After the war he continued his career as a journalist and gained fame as a writer for children.

Robert Nichols (1893–1944)

Educated at Winchester and Trinity College, Oxford, which he left after a year. He was a close friend of Brooke and Sassoon before the outbreak of war. He was commissioned in the Royal Field Artillery and fought on the Somme, but was invalided out with shell shock.

From 1921 to 1924 he was Professor of English at Tokyo University.

Wilfred Owen (1893–1918)

Born in Oswestry and educated at Birkenhead Institute and Shrewsbury Technical School. From 1911 to 1913 he was a lay assistant to the Vicar of Dunsden in Oxfordshire. In 1915 he returned from a tutorial post in France and enlisted in the Artists' Rifles. Later, as a lieutenant in the Manchester Regiment he served in the trenches on the Somme from January to June 1917. He was invalided home with neurasthenia and convalesced at Craiglockhart Hospital, Edinburgh, where he was influenced, advised and encouraged by Siegfried Sassoon. Much of his best poetry was written at Scarborough between September 1917 and October 1918.

Returning to active service on the Western Front, he was awarded the Military Cross in October 1918. He was killed on 4 November 1918, seven days before the end of the war, while leading his company across the Sambre Canal. He is acknowledged by most critics to be the outstanding poet of the war.

Herbert Read (1893–1968)

Born and brought up in Yorkshire. His law studies at Leeds University were interrupted by the war. He became an officer in the Green Howards and fought on the Western Front gaining the D.S.O. and M.C. in the process. After the war, he held many academic posts and was knighted in 1953.

E. A. Rickword (1898–1982)

Joined the Artists' Rifles straight from school in 1916, and then transferred to the Royal Berkshire Regiment. He was awarded the Military Cross, but was invalided out having lost an eye.

Isaac Rosenberg (1890–1916)

The son of poor Lithuanian Jewish parents, he was born in Bristol and brought up in the East End of London. He left school at the age of 14, later entering the Slade School of Art, due to the generosity of some Jewish patrons. Then he went to South Africa, hoping the climate would improve his weak lungs, but returned to England in 1915 and enlisted in a Bantam Battalion. He was entirely unsuited to army life, being absent-minded and clumsy, and mingling with ordinary soldiers, some of whom did not sympathize with his artistic nature. He wrote much of his finest poetry on scraps of paper in awful trench conditions. He was killed in action on the Somme on 1 April 1918, during the great German advance.

Siegfried Sassoon (1886–1967)

Born into a wealthy Jewish banking family. He was educated at Marlborough and Clare College, Cambridge, which he left without taking a degree. Before the war, he devoted himself to a life of hunting, cricket, opera and literature. He joined the army on the first day of the war, and on his arrival at the Somme front with the Royal Welch

Fusiliers rapidly acquired a reputation for reckless bravery, earning the nickname 'Mad Jack', and a Military Cross.

By February 1917, he began to question the diplomatic motives for continuing the war, and after meeting famous pacifists at Garsington Manor, near Oxford, sent a strongly worded statement to the newspapers and to his commanding officer. He was saved from a court martial by his friend Robert Graves, who claimed Sassoon was suffering from a nervous breakdown. He was sent to Craiglockhart Hospital, Edinburgh, where he recovered under the care of Dr W. H. Rivers. Wilfred Owen was a fellow patient who was given significant guidance and encouragement by Sassoon.

In February 1918 he was sent to Egypt and then back to France. On 18 July 1918, while returning from a patrol, he was shot in the head by a British sentry and spent the rest of the war recovering in hospital.

After the war he gained fame as the author of outstanding works such as *Memoirs of a Fox-hunting Man* and *Memoirs of an Infantry Officer*.

R. H. Sauter

Published *Songs in Captivity* in 1922. The poems contained in this book imply that he was interned in Britain for four years until after the Armistice.

Alan Seeger (1888–1916)

Born in New York and later spent some time living a Bohemian existence in Paris. On the outbreak of war he joined the French Foreign Legion, fighting in the Champagne and Somme Fronts, where he was killed on 4 July 1916.

C. H. Sorley (1895–1915)

Educated at Marlborough and then enlisted in the Suffolk Regiment instead of taking up his scholarship to Oxford. He was shot by a sniper while leading his company into the attack on 13 October 1915 during the Battle of Loos.

Many literary critics feel that next to Wilfred Owen he was the most promising of the young poets killed in the war.

J. C. Squire (1884–1958)

Educated at Blundells and Cambridge, he became the literary editor of the *New Statesman* in 1913. He was unfit for active service, but supported the war effort, with great sympathy for the ordinary soldier.

Edward Thomas (1876–1917)

Educated at St. Paul's and Lincoln College, Oxford. He earned his living before the war as a reviewer and essayist. Having enlisted in the Artists' Rifles in 1915, he was then commissioned as a second lieutenant in the Royal Garrison Artillery in 1916. He wrote only a few war poems, concentrating on nature and the countryside as his usual themes, before he was killed at Arras in April 1917.

R. E. Vernède (1875–1917)

Educated at St Paul's and Oxford. He enlisted in the ranks of the Fusiliers in September 1914 and was then commissioned into the Rifle Brigade in 1915. He was wounded during the Battle of the Somme (1916), but insisted on returning to the Front. He was killed while leading an attack on Havrincourt Wood on 9 April 1917.

**Arthur Graeme West
(1891–1917)**

Educated at Blundells and Oxford, he enlisted as a private in the Public Schools' Battalion in February 1915 and soon came to hate army life. He rose to the rank of captain in the Oxford and Bucks Light Infantry. He was killed on 3 April 1917.

**T. P. Cameron Wilson
(1889–1918)**

A Derbyshire schoolmaster who enlisted in the Grenadier Guards as a private, later transferring to the Sherwood Foresters, where he rose to staff captain. He was killed in action on the Somme on 23 March 1918.

Acknowledgements

For permission to reprint copyright material the publishers gratefully acknowledge the following:

Rosica Colin Ltd for 'Field Manoeuvres', 'Soliloquy 2', 'Proem', by Richard Aldington; Mrs Nicolete Gray and The Society of Authors on behalf of the Laurence Binyon Estate for 'For the Fallen (September 1914)' by Laurence Binyon; A. D. Peters & Co Ltd for 'Concert Party: Busseboom', 'The Watchers' by Edmund Blunden (reprinted by permission); Mr Michael Gibson and Macmillan, London and Basingstoke for 'Back', 'Breakfast', 'The Conscript' from *Collected Poems 1905–25* by W. W. Gibson; Methuen & Co for 'In the Gallery Where the Fat Men Go' from *The Sorrows of War* by Louis Golding; A. P. Watt Ltd on behalf of the Executors of the Estate of Robert Graves for 'The Dead Foxhunter' and 'Two Fusiliers', and for 'Goliath and David' from *Collected Poems 1975*; the *New Statesman* for 'High Wood' by Philip Johnstone (from *The Nation*, 16 February 1918); *Punch* for 'In Flanders Field' by John McCrae; Curtis Brown Ltd, London, on behalf of the Milne Estate for 'Gold Braid' by A. A. Milne; the estate of Robert Nichols and Chatto & Windus for 'Noon' from *Ardours and Endurances* by Robert Nichols; the estate of the author, the editor and the Hogarth Press for 'Dulce et Decorum Est', 'Anthem for Doomed Youth', 'Disabled', 'Apologia Pro Poemate Meo', 'Exposure', 'Strange Meeting', 'The Parable of the Old Men and the Young' from *The Collected Poems of Wilfred Owen* edited by Jon Stallworthy; Carcanet Press Ltd for 'Winter Warfare' from *Behind the Eyes* by Edgell Rickword; Faber & Faber Ltd and David Higham Associates for 'My Men Go Wearily' from *Poems 1914–1918* by Herbert Read; George Sassoon for 'Aftermath', 'Attack', 'Base Details', 'Blighters', 'Counter Attack', 'The Death-Bed', 'Does it Matter?' 'The Dug Out', 'Fight to a Finish', 'The General', 'Glory of Women', 'The Redeemer', 'Suicide in the Trenches', 'To Any Dead Officer', 'A Working Party' by Siegfried Sassoon; Mrs Myfanwy Thomas and Faber & Faber for 'As the Team's Head Brass' from *Collected Poems* by Edward Thomas.

While every effort has been made to secure permission, in some cases it has proved impossible to trace the copyright holders. The publishers apologise for this apparent negligence.

For permission to reproduce illustrations the publishers gratefully acknowledge the Imperial War Museum, who supplied all the photographs except the photograph on page 62, which was supplied by the *East Anglian Daily Times*.

Index of First Lines

Edward Hudson is greatly indebted to a number of friends and acquaintances who have helped him to compile the anthology. In particular to Janet Padbury, Enid Volak, Joy Rummey, Sybil Hudson, Sue Duff, Barbara Barron, D. P. Devitt, R. K. Ingram, M. J. Harrison and M. W. A. Gover. The staff of the photographic department of the Imperial War Museum, and in particular, Mr M. Willis. Dominic Hibberd for his tolerance in coping with endless questions. Mrs Anne Powell of Palladour Books who provided detailed answers to seemingly impossible questions. Jon Stallworthy for his eternally good humoured guidance. And finally, to his wife, Jane.

STOCKPORT GRAMMAR SCHOOL
LIBRARY.